# A Gorgeous Sexy Life

by brenda hawbaker lewis

Library of Congress Cataloging-in-Publication Data

ISBN:978-1-7352083-0-5

Printed in the United States of America

Special thanks to "Mommy," "Sir," and my wonderful family who are "love personified," to Carolyn Christmann for graciously lavishing her editing talents on this book, and most of all to Timmy and those like him for inspiring and challenging me to live a more gorgeous sexy life!

.

# Introduction

Why I wrote a book about my brother Timmy

I can't remember when my brother Timmy first used the words "gorgeous and sexy" to describe a cup of coffee or the myriad of other things he loves. But, this has always been his favorite phrase to praise something he enjoyed: "gorgeous and sexy." For Timmy, it has nothing to do with sexiness or looks, but everything to do with appreciating the simple goodness of life. It's just the way Timmy perceives the world.

I realize, for most of us, the world is anything but gorgeous and sexy. Political upheaval, social and financial anxieties, and family stresses are often the norm. But Timmy is blissfully unaware of the things that keep others awake at night. He lives a life of gratitude and seems to maintain infinite joy in the midst of chaos. I don't possess those qualities as much as I'd like, but as Timmy's sister, I've had a front row seat in watching Timmy live out his life values: loving God and loving others beautifully.

Timmy was born into our family with a genetic syndrome called Fragile X (a genetic mutation carried on the X chromosome). Women carry the syndrome and are seldom affected by it, yet men who receive the gene almost always possess the developmental challenges associated with it. My immediate family is a textbook example: half of the siblings received the chromosome from our mother and half did not. Neither I nor my younger sister Connie inherited the gene. Pam, the first born, is a carrier of Fragile X but not affected by it, and then Timmy received it fully.

Long before geneticists discovered Fragile X in 1991, we knew something was awry in our family tree. But, we didn't know what it was or how it wove its way through our branches so thoroughly. We just knew that so many of the boys in our family were impacted by some sort of genetic anomaly that made them "different."

But, even after Fragile X was identified, our understanding of the gene was limited. Early on, my sister Connie and I would, half-jokingly, blame being forgetful on Fragile X. We would leave our keys in the fridge or forget someone's name and say, "It must be the X!" Ironically, these situations were actually signs we didn't have the gene. Fragile X affected people are very aware of everything and everyone around them.

The Fragile X gene is everywhere in the family tree – my brother, my cousins, and my uncles. In fact, when scientists first discovered the gene, they did one of the early studies on my family. Because it came from our great-grandfather, we were told that it looked like we were a greenhouse for "growing mentally disabled boys." When I was young we would travel with our Fragile X children and people would always stare at us. I didn't understand why at the time, because for me, it was normal. Later on, I realized that to the outside world, we probably looked as if we were leading a mentally challenged group home vacation!

Over the years, well meaning people would often point out that our family must have a terrible "burden to bear." But we don't feel burdened. There is a movement among families with mentally disabled children called "The Lucky Few." And, that truly is the way we feel. We are among the lucky few who have had the privilege of raising a "special" child.

The special children of our family are the – sometimes needy, but most of the time beautiful – glue that seems to permeate everything. And just like glue, they have helped hold all of us together. We have shared funny stories and learned profound truths through Timmy and our other special family members. This is not an attempt to put an optimistic spin on a difficult situation. Along with special joys, there are extreme challenges. There are many intellectual and physical things that can be almost impossible for these children, like reading, driving, or even tying their own shoes. There are jobs they can never accomplish, education they will never achieve, and understanding that will never be attained.

Our Fragile X boys are developmentally delayed and mentally challenged in every area, except in giving love. Many special children have mental abilities of a 5–7-year-old child. Most will never be able to live alone, navigate a computer, read a book, or get married. Timmy will always live with our mother (who he calls "Mommy"), and our father (who he calls "Sir"), in Fort Myers, Florida.

Timmy, like all Fragile X children, will remain an eternal child.

Yet, these children feel deeply, love fully, and understand far more than the casual observer might perceive. I wrote this book so that you, the reader, could meet Timmy through his stories. While Timmy has some mental challenges, he seems to excel in the parts of life that really matter. He loves and serves people better than just about anyone I know, better than me for sure!

I often ask myself the internal question: "Who is mentally disabled, Timmy or me?" If God measures us by our unconditional love and value of others, Timmy is the "normal" one, and the rest of us are delayed in our development. Is Timmy perfect? No. Does he get frustrated and upset? Of course! He is not Jesus. But he has shown me more of Jesus than just about anyone else on Earth. I hope that this book represents Timmy well and that in reading it, you can share in the inspiration and joy he brings to our family and to all who know him!

Welcome to the gorgeous, sexy life of my brother,

Timothy Lynn Hawbaker.

Timmy through the years

# Timmy's Take on Helping Others

# "Sure! I will do that for you!"

is Timmy's usual response when asked to do even the most mundane task. Timmy, can you carry this big suitcase? "Sure!" Timmy can you help me wash the car? "Sure! Of course I will." Timmy works hard serving people all day. He doesn't sit down very often. He washes dishes. He cares for his Pomeranian dog, Roxi. He makes "gorgeous, sexy" coffee and tea. He helps Mommy, Sir, and anyone else who asks all day long.

And if you ask him why he works so hard, he'll simply say, "I don't want to be lazy, you know. Someone's gotta do it!"

# "B Jean didn't make her bed!"

Timmy's work ethic is especially activated when it comes to an unmade bed, which means I'm in trouble every time he comes to visit. Inevitably, he will pass by my room, spot my tousled bed, and with unveiled offense, announce,
"B. Jean (Timmy's name for me) didn't make her bed! Do you believe that Mommy? She didn't even make her bed!!! It looks all messy!"

And yet, later on in the night, when I walk into my room tired and sleepy, I will find my bed beautifully made, courtesy of Timmy. He never tells me he did it or expects any thanks or gratitude. In Timmy's world, a messy bed must be made!

# "My legs aren't broken,"

Timmy quipped when I brought him a lemonade not too long ago. It's a common phrase for Timmy. As much as he likes to serve, he's not so keen on being served. In fact, I can't recall a single time he has asked me to do anything for him, ever. He doesn't request help, because he doesn't want it. And if you try anyway, you'll most likely be met with a snarky comment or his hasty departure.

The same applies to acknowledging his serving. If you thank or praise him too much, he'll sidestep it by saying something sarcastic to get you off the subject of himself. He doesn't want accolades. He simply wants to do things to make life easier for those he loves. And, since his legs aren't broken, that's exactly what he does, always!

# "I saved the groceries!"

If there is an errand that needs to be run, Timmy's always there, ready to help. As such, our grandfather would often take Timmy along on his trips to the store. One day, as Gram-Pa and Timmy drove back from the local market, Timmy noticed the car in front of them had come to a complete stop.

But Gram-Pa wasn't slowing down! With urgency, Timmy began repeating, "We are gonna wreck, Gram-Pa. We are gonna wreck!" But Gram-Pa, whose reflexes were slowing, didn't respond. He didn't hit the brakes.

Anticipating the imminent wreck, Timmy took matters into his own hands. He grabbed the groceries and Gram-Pa's cane, opened the door, and jumped out of the car just seconds before the impact.

Crash! The cars collided just as Timmy had warned. Gram-Pa and Timmy were both ok, but taken to the hospital for observation.

When my Mother arrived, she found Gram-Pa laying in the hospital bed, with Timmy sitting in the chair next to him, still holding fast to the groceries and Gram-Pa's cane. "Ut, I told him to stop!" Timmy explained. "He just kept on going. But, I saved the groceries, Mommy!"

# "I'm as strong as an ox, you know!"

And, Timmy just might be! He can lift and carry almost anything. As our family grows older – and age impacts our bodies and abilities – we rely on Timmy's strength more and more. A need that Timmy is happy to fulfill. He loves to help us lift or move things, from bags to boxes to chairs and sofas, although if too large or heavy, he may declare "this is awkwasness".

Christmas is especially fun for Timmy because he gets to go shopping with the girls. No matter how many stores we visit or hours it takes, he never gets tired of lugging all the gifts. And, of all the men in our family, he definitely wins the best shopper award, both for his endurance and sweet attitude while doing it!

# "Sure, I'm not too tired!"

When it comes to carrying, and caring, for the babies in our extended family, Timmy has extra strength and sensitivity. He has helped care for every one of his nieces and nephews (and now their children), and many times he's been the only one able to calm and rock them to sleep.

Whenever we're out walking or hiking, the smallest children always beg to be carried by Timmy. He would rather his arms fall off than to disappoint his little ones. Usually, an adult tries to come to his rescue, saying, "Timmy your arms must be tired. You can put them down." He'll comply "with tough love", telling the child, "You can walk. Your feet aren't broken." But minutes later, inevitably they'll ask to be carried again, and Timmy always says, "Sure! I'm not too tired."

# "Of course I will... I can do that for you!"

When young, the children in our family see Timmy as a sure source of comfort. But as they get older, they notice Timmy's differences. "He's funny!" they'll say, or "Timmy has a funny voice." They also quickly learn that because Timmy wants everyone to be happy, he's easy to manipulate into doing just about anything they want.

If your Mom and Dad say no to another cookie? Ask Timmy. He'll surely say, "I'll get that for you!" When Mom and Dad are too tired for another bedtime book, ask Timmy. Although he doesn't read, he'll always say "Of course!" Then he will rock them – turning the pages of a children's book and telling them Timmy-invented stories to match the pictures – until they finally fall fast asleep.

Timmy's family: the Hawbaker clan

# Timmy's Take on Valuing People

# "Hi Steve! What ya been up to... still building houses?"

When Timmy meets people, he always greets them by name and tells them it was nice to see them. He is quick with a handshake or hug as well, sometimes surprising people who don't come from physically affectionate families. But a Timmy hug can make anyone melt!

Not only does Timmy greet people by name, but he also remembers details about their lives. "Hi Sue, how is Doug doin? Heard he got a new car. Woo Hoo!". His recall and questions affirm and value the people he encounters. He never read the book "How to Win Friends and Influence People" and doesn't need to. The principle is embedded in his nature. As a result, Timmy is pretty much the most popular person anywhere he goes. If you ever take a stroll with him, you'll feel as though you are walking with a celebrity. Timmy knows and loves everybody and, as a result, has quite a big fan club.

# "You're gonna have a baby in November? Woo Hoo!"

One time, Timmy, Mommy, and Sir came to visit me in New Haven, Connecticut. I was living there in a Christian community called Youth with a Mission/Axiom. At our weekly community gathering, I introduced Timmy to Austin and told him that he was married to Erika and that they were expecting a baby in November.

Austin and Timmy spoke for a few minutes and then Timmy went on to meet and chat with dozens of other people in the room. Later, when Timmy was introduced to Austin's wife, he said "nice to meet you Erika! You are married to Austin. I met your gorgeous husband in the living room. And, you are going to have a baby in November? Woo Hoo!"

# "You can cook for me any day!"

This is Timmy's way of showing his gratitude for any and every meal he enjoys, whether it be McDonalds, someone's home cooking, or an upscale restaurant. Often, he'll surprise the waiters or servers with his exclamation of gratitude, "You can cook for me any day!"

And no matter how often he enjoys somebody's culinary gifts, he makes sure to appreciate them every time. Our sister Pam, who got all the cooking DNA in our family, gets Timmy's praise the most, especially when she makes her special chocolate chip cookies. "You can make cookies for me any day!" Timmy will declare every … single … time.

# "She loves yellow"

Timmy loves observing and describing people. When he says or hears someone's name, he'll usually add a custom Timmy description, such as: Liz "Jordan's pretty wife," Jim See "Everybody loves Jim See," or Jordan "he used to be a bachelor like me." Ricci is simply "that crazy woman," and her daughter Olivia, "she sure can sing." Kaley, "she dances here, she dances there," and Jim, "he's a big tall farmer, you know." Connie, "she works all the time," and Janet, "she loves yellow!" Almost everyone he knows has a description.

For those Timmy knows and loves well, the descriptions are like a verbal caricature, highlighting our obvious traits, but not always the ones we prefer to be known for. When Mommy mentioned my name recently, Timmy smiled and called me the "mountain nut!" Timmy's descriptions are never done in malice. What Timmy "sees" and describes so well are sometimes those things the rest of us fail to notice.

Timmy, Mommy, and Sir in Florida

# Timmy's Take on Marriage and Sex

# "Women cost too much!"

This is Timmy's favorite response when asked why he's not married. His bachelorhood has become a badge of honor for him. He is happy to choose the simple life over the trap of materialism called marriage. It's an opinion most likely formed by having observed the shopping habits of the women in his life. Having only sisters, he has seen our propensity for purchasing things – make-up, clothes, jewelry, shoes!

Of course, it is not just the financial costs that Timmy is talking about. All of us Hawbaker ladies, including our mother, are by nature a bit high maintenance. From an early age, Timmy noticed that we girls seemed to be "needier" than him in every way. Plus, Timmy hates emotional outbursts, and, with four women in the house, large displays of feelings were quite common. Timmy probably decided that a Mom and three sisters were quite enough women to take care of!

# "Women make you build houses!"

From floor plans to paint colors, Timmy has witnessed the time, money, and stress involved in the building process ... more than once. Our sister Connie and her husband built ten homes over the course of their marriage. Watching these "ordeals," Timmy deduced that if there was no wife in his life, he wouldn't need to build them a home, and no house building equals no stress, so he's definitely better off as a bachelor!

# "People marry to keep each other warm!"

Though Timmy is content as a bachelor, his answer to why people get married always seems to make women sigh and swoon. "People marry to keep each other warm!" he'll declare. No one ever told him that answer. He just decided it made sense…and perhaps it does. Having someone to hold you and keep you warm when the world can seem so cold, seems like a good reason to marry!

# "I am warm enough!"

If marriage is made to keep people warm, then Timmy is quick to explain that he is quite warm enough, thank you! Mommy, Sir, and Roxy (his little Pomeranian dog) keep him quite comfortable, so he has no plans of heading to the altar. He is committed to bachelorhood, unlike those obviously very "cold" guys in the family who need someone to keep them warm.

# "Stop your cryin' woman ... just ship him down the river!"

Many years ago I went through a devastating divorce. Throughout the many months of grief and pain, Timmy was right there, comforting, serving, and being available. I couldn't stop the tears. They were constant, and so was Timmy. He stayed by my side through all the tissues, talking, sobbing, and talking some more.

But, when Timmy has had enough, he is done. One day, as the tears started rolling again, Timmy said, "Stop your cryin, would ya, woman? I would ship him down the river!" Somehow, the tears turned to laughter. His tough love was comforting. Timmy was right. Maybe, I had cried enough.

# "Big, fat, juicy lips"

If Timmy is watching a movie and a kissing scene gets a little too hot and heavy, he turns his head away in embarrassment. And, if you even mention the word sex, he'll quickly chastise you, "We don't talk about that … its too embarrassing!"

But Timmy gets crushes on beautiful women just like the next guy. He used to keep a picture of Cindy Crawford on his dresser. He said she had "big fat juicy lips" and still uses that phrase to describe any woman he finds attractive. But though he appreciates the beauty of "juicy lips," he's completely childlike when it comes to the idea of physical intimacy.

# "Oh, Connie would never do that!"

Many years ago, Timmy overheard a group of women discussing the infertility issues of our younger sister, Connie. One woman jokingly said, "I wonder if they have tried sex?" For Timmy, sex is a subject way too embarrassing to talk or even think about. Upon hearing the women's remark, Timmy just had to intervene. He turned to them and emphatically stated, "Oh Connie would never do that!" (Eventually it all worked out, and God blessed Connie and her husband with two wonderful children.)

# "Pregnant! I'm not even married!"

Every year, Mommy takes Timmy with her to the drugstore to get his seasonal flu shot. One year, the receptionist filling out the paperwork must have been on "autopilot," as he went through the same questionnaire with each customer. Without looking up, he asked Timmy, "are you pregnant?" Exasperated, Timmy replied, "Pregnant! I'm not even married!" The pharmacist looked up quite shocked to see Timmy standing there.

# "You married her."

Timmy is not a fan of arguments of any kind. When it comes to marital disputes, Timmy's response reminds the offended spouse of the obvious, but easy-to-forget, truth: their partner was their choice. If a wife is frustrated with her husband, he'll say, "Well, you married him!" And if a husband is angry at his wife, he'll say, "You married her." According to Timmy, you chose to marry them, so you might as well just choose to get along!

The Hawbaker 6 on the church steps
(Easter Sunday, 1962)

# Timmy's Take on God and Heaven

# "Thank you Jesus!"

When Timmy is trying to accomplish a really difficult task, he almost always calls on Jesus for help, and when he completes the job, he gives credit where credit is due, saying "Thank you Lord!"

One warm Spring day, when our Gram-Pa could no longer walk alone, he told Timmy that he would give anything to take a simple stroll down the street. To which Timmy replied, "OK, I'll take you, Gram-Pa!" Timmy hoisted him up, resting most of Gram-Pa's weight on his back. They shuffled inch by inch down the street and back, for over an hour, both grinning ear to ear. Returning home, Timmy eased Gram-Pa into his chair, flopped onto the couch, and breathed an exhausted but grateful, "Whew! Thank you Jesus!"

# "Ask the BIG MAN upstairs!"

Timmy doesn't talk about God much, but his faith is evident in action. Often I'll "interview" Timmy to get his unique views on life and all sorts of topics. One time, I asked him what he thought about Jesus dying on the cross for us. To which he replied, "I don't know … why are ya talkin to me? Ask the BIG MAN upstairs!" If you have questions about faith, Timmy knows exactly where to direct you. "Take it to the Lord's house!"

# "They need to go to the Lord's house!"

According to Timmy, it's not only questions that should take you to the Lord's house. If Timmy sees someone smoking, cussing, drinking, or packing on too much PDA, he'll emphatically declare, "They need to go to the Lord's house!" He'll also use this phrase when he hears about anyone's bad behavior … even if it comes from the nightly news.

One time, he was ready to send our whole family to the Lord's house for an indiscretion with alcohol. We were having a family communion service and forgot to tell Timmy that the sacrament was real wine, rather than the grape juice that he was accustomed to. When the cup passed to Timmy and he took a sip, shock flashed over his face. Aghast, he exclaimed, "I think this wine has been spiked!"

# "How rude of me!"

One Sunday at church, Timmy inadvertently walked by an old family friend without saying "hi." When the friend teasingly admonished him about it, Timmy's response was immediate, "how rude of me!"

If you confront Timmy about a wrongdoing or give him correction (which doesn't happen often), he's never defensive. Rather, he takes the humble route. "Timmy, did you say that I talk too much?" "Timmy, did you forget to hug me?" "How rude of me!" he'll say.

# "Who'd want to see that old dead thing?"

A few years back, our dog Macy – who had been in the family for more than eight years – got sick suddenly and died. We were all very sad and buried her in the yard with a doggie funeral. Later that night, as we reminisced about our beloved pet, someone asked Timmy, "Wouldn't you love to see Macy right now?" Timmy looked at us incredulously and said, "Who'd want to see that old dead thing?"

# "He's dead, you know!"

Before a church service a couple of years ago, Mommy was consoling a bereaved widow on the unexpected passing of her husband. As they spoke, Timmy walked up and interjected, "he's dead, you know!" With great concern, our mother began apologizing for Timmy's comment, but the widow just smiled and said, "It's ok. He's right after all." For Timmy, death is not a sensitive topic to be avoided, but a reality of life. Heaven seems to be a thin boundary for Timmy. He is not separated from God by a thick wall, but a translucent veil he seems to see through.

# "See ya later, Gramma!"

Our Grandmother died many years ago. At her funeral, as is tradition, the family stood around the open coffin, crying and soothing ourselves with the usual sentiments, "Doesn't she look peaceful?" "Doesn't she look good?" Pleasantries that we don't really mean, but seem to console us nonetheless. As we stood there, Timmy walked up to the casket, glanced down, and said, "See ya later Gramma." Then he turned and walked away. Timmy's simple and absolute trust in heaven gave him complete confidence that he would see Gramma again.

# "Oh well, nobody got Killed!"

Like many in our family, our sister Connie often asks Timmy to accompany her to the grocery store. Once, while backing out of the driveway, she crashed into her brother-in-law's convertible car. Distraught, she sobbed, "I just don't know how I did that, Timmy!" Timmy, on the other hand, remained calm. He just looked at her and replied matter-of-factly, "It's ok, Connie. Nobody got killed."

Timmy puts hard circumstances into better perspective for all of us. We've all since adopted his phrase as a reality check when something bad happens in the family. "Someone stole your bike?" "Your checkbook's overdrawn?"..."Oh well, nobody got killed!"

# Timmy with some of

hulk hands

characters

birthday gifts

biking with the night riders

# the " things " he loves

stuffed animals

hiking with his family

taking care of roxie

trains and everything about them

Timmy on his three-wheeler

# Timmy's Take on Life's Simple Pleasures

# "It was sorta fun, you know."

When Timmy was a teenager, our family took one of our many vacations to Colorado. On this particular trip, Sir had been planning to drive to the top of Pikes Peak, throw a Frisbee, and watch it fly down to the valley below. He'd been talking about it for weeks and was thrilled when the day finally arrived. We reached the summit, found the right spot, and he put the Frisbee down to make the final preparations.

As Sir readied his camera to catch the momentous occasion, he spotted, out of the corner of his eye, Timmy picking up the Frisbee. He pleaded "No Timmy! No Timmy! No Timmy!" But it was too late. The Frisbee, and fun, went soaring out of Timmy's hands into the valley far below, leaving Dad with a mournful, "Ohhhhhh Timmy!" "It was sorta fun you know," was Timmy's only explanation.

Over the years, this story of the fateful Frisbee event has been repeated hundreds of times, and it still makes both Sir and Timmy smile.

# "Sure … I always sleep well!"

Our family is full of night owls, so when we're all together, there are always games, snacks, and conversations well into the evening. Timmy joins in the fun until 9:00 p.m. on the dot. Then suddenly, he disappears. That's it. Lights out. Goodnight. No announcement or fanfare. Timmy just tucks himself into bed and quickly falls asleep.

He never struggles with insomnia or waking at night with worries or frets. A day well spent deserves a good night's rest. And every morning, Timmy's very accurate internal alarm clock wakes him at 6:00 am, ready for another day of helping and playing. If you ask if he slept well, the answer is always the same, "Sure, I always do!"

# "Smash … smash it down!"

For Timmy, chores are rarely chore-ish. He delights in helping around the house and usually enjoys the task itself, especially when it comes to the garbage. Whenever he sorts the recycling or takes out the trash, he relishes the act of crunching the garbage into the bins to make room for more, and it's always done with extra-enthusiastic and contagious sound effects… "CURUUUNCH! Smash it dowwwwwwn!" I can never take my own garbage out without loudly and energetically "smashing it down!"

# "It flushes good!"

Timmy reported when he rejoined us outside the restaurant. We had waited awhile for him, but we were never worried. We all knew exactly where Timmy was: surveying the flushing merits of the toilets, as is his unique habit at any and every truck stop, gas station, church, or private home.

Timmy just loves flushing toilets. Whether he actually needs to use the restroom or not, whenever we arrive at a new place, he'll jump out of the car and head straight for the bathroom. We are not exactly sure why; perhaps it's the appeal of the flushing sound, or maybe it's a litmus test of a nice clean facility. It may be a tough habit for germaphobes to fathom, but the act of flushing toilets makes Timmy very happy.

# "I hear ya, rooster!"

Timmy's ability to validate and appreciate doesn't stop with humans or even living things. He's aware of every sound and likes to acknowledge its source. The teapot whines, "I hear ya, teapot." Roxy barks to go on a walk, "I hear you, beast." An ambulance siren screams toward us, "I hear ya, ambulance!" Any noticeable sounds, especially if they are loud, will bring an enthusiastic acknowledgement from Timmy. A rooster is crowing, "I hear ya, rooster!"

# "I'm not gonna get large!"

Timmy has a dear friend who loves food. Once, as they shared lunch together, Timmy's friend explained how he needed to lose some weight for his health, to which Timmy suggested, "You eat too much." Timmy's been known to give this same unsolicited advice to anyone having trouble saying no to food. Such a statement from most people would surely cause a problem. But, when Timmy says it, people howl with laughter, acknowledging the truth of his words.

Timmy also holds himself to the same standard. He doesn't often overeat. When tempted to have an extra cookie, even his sister Pam's beloved chocolate chip one, he declines by saying, "I don't want to get large, you know?!"

# "I wrapped it myself!"

Timmy loves to give gifts, and it's always easy to spot a Timmy present. Just look for duct tape … lots of it! Timmy insists on wrapping all of his gifts himself, and he always uses his very special wrapping technique: the more tape and layers the better.

Christmas of 2017 was particularly memorable. Timmy was very excited to wrap his gift for Sir. First, he placed the present into a plastic bag and then covered it in duct tape. Then, another bag. Then more duct tape. Bag. Duct tape. Bag. Duct tape. Repeat. It took 45 minutes for Sir to unwrap that gift! The rest of the family enjoyed the presentation almost as much as Timmy. None of us can remember the gift, but we can never forget the wrapping!

# "I bet that's been there ever since it was built!"

Not having a reference for distance, height, or age, Timmy's measurements are one of a kind. For instance, when Timmy and Mommy were driving past the old courthouse one day, Timmy observed, "I bet that's been there ever since it was built!"

Timmy likes traveling, but he doesn't like long road trips. If he thinks the distance is too far, he'll tell you, "The road is just too long!"

"Whoa, Kaley … your legs go all the way to the floor!", Timmy marveled to his niece when he saw her after a recent growth spurt. Hearing this, Kaley's brother Colby asked, "Timmy, do my legs go all the way to the floor?" To which Timmy quickly replied, "Oh … not yet, Colby!"

Timmy posing on a family vacation in Hawaii

# Timmy's Take on Valuing Himself and His Abilities

# "I put my name on it!"

If you spend any time with Timmy, you're apt to notice Timmy's sweet signature on all of his belongings. He puts his name on everything he owns: his beach towel, his cooler, his collections, his bike. For Timmy, labeling is not just about ownership, but also stewardship. Timmy takes exceptional care of everything he has. But that doesn't mean he won't share. He'll lend you his possessions, even though he has a hunch that you won't take care of it like he would.

And for Timmy, labeling goes both ways. If you leave your Coke lying around, you may return to find an empty glass. Timmy tries to moderate his soda intake, but he really loves a cold Coke. If he's thirsty, and there's an unlabeled cup of cola around, he's most likely going to guzzle it down. When you notice your glass is empty, he'll never lie or deny. He'll just say "Sure was good!" And his only justification: "Did it have your name on it? I don't think so."

# "I was plum embarrassed!"

Timmy loves his nieces and nephews, but if we are out in public, and one of them throws a tantrum, all bets are off. He will promptly act as if he doesn't know us, walk to the far end of the store, and make himself busy, straightening clothes or arranging canned goods as if he was an employee. If there is no distracting task at hand, he will just walk as fast and far away as possible.

Big public displays of emotion – especially negative ones like anger or frustration – are embarrassing to Timmy. He doesn't put up with that type of behavior in himself or anyone else. His only defense is just to leave. Later, he will tell Mommy, "I was plum embarrassed!"

# "You gotta be smart like me!"

Once, when Timmy saw me struggling to carry old chairs a block to the recycling center, he said, "you do it like this, B Jean," and proceeded to stack all four chairs on his three-wheeler bike and finish the job in half the time. I said, "Timmy, how did you do that?" He very confidently replied, "you gotta be smart like me."

Timmy doesn't think in abstracts and, as a result, is brilliant in practical day-to-day living. And, when it comes to recalling details, Timmy is a genius! Our Dad (Sir), used to fly small airplanes. Whenever Timmy came with him to the airport, Sir would quiz Timmy, asking him to identify the type of airplane by the sound of its engine while flying, and 99% of the time, Timmy would know the answer!

# "It's probably where you left it!"

We all have a tendency to lose things: cell phones, keys, purses, coats, etc. But not Timmy, whose memory always seems to be in "scan mode," observing and recalling where everything is. "Oh Tim, I have lost my phone!" "It's in the bedroom I imagine," Timmy replies. But there's no imagining about it. Timmy knows for sure the phone is absolutely and positively in the bedroom. "Timmy, where is my purse?" "It's by the front door, I think." Or, if he feels like giving us a hard time, he may tease, "it's probably where you left it!"

# "Your legs aren't broken, are they?"

Timmy works hard, but he knows his limits. At the end of a long day, when Timmy is physically exhausted, he is "done" and can rarely be persuaded to do more. Even then, if asked, he tends to avoid saying "no," but rather replies, "My bones are too tired." Sometimes, if he is really exhausted, he'll shift the responsibility back on the asker, using one of his favorite phrases, "Your legs aren't broken, are they?"

Life's a beach!

# Timmy's Take on Finances
# and What's Valuable

# "I bet that cost five thousand dolla's"

For Timmy, that's the cost of anything he finds of value: a sofa, a new shirt, a house, or even an ink pen. Many years ago, Mommy had a rummage sale and Timmy was selling a small pair of weights. Mommy labeled the weights at a bargain $5.00 and was surprised that, by the end of the day, they still hadn't sold. Until she noticed the price tag! Unbeknownst to any of us, Timmy added three zeros, to make sure the buyers knew the weight set's true value: $5,000 of course!

# "Money? It ain't cheap, you Know!"

is what Timmy says if you are talking about finances. Everyone knows if you are going to give Timmy money, he would much rather have ten single dollar bills over one $10, because obviously it is better to have more bills in your wallet!

Timmy calls it "Moolah" and will oftentimes use the gesture – one hand brushing the palm of the other – as he exclaims, "woo hoo … I got lots of dollas!" However, lack of money never caused Timmy a moment of worry. Perhaps it's one of the reasons he has aged so well, with so few wrinkles. If Timmy has a couple of dollars in his wallet, he is truly a happy man!

# "I'll give you SIX!"

A few years ago, Timmy, Uncle Billy, and the rest of our extended family headed to Juarez Mexico for vacation. Uncle Billy, who is also affected by Fragile X, learned that it was customary to bargain with shopkeepers in the market. When he found a belt he wanted, he asked the shopkeeper how much it cost. The gentleman said, "Five Dollars." With aplomb, Billy countered, "I'll give you six!" The shop owner quickly accepted that deal and everyone, including Uncle Billy, walked away happy!

# "What would I need a house for?"

If you offer Timmy a new house, he'd most likely decline with a candid, "What would I need a house for?" The offer of a car might provoke a similar response. "I don't drive!" He has no use for those big things, but boy do his eyes light up if you give him a new toy or DVD.

If you go shopping with Timmy, you'll be treated to an ongoing commentary about whatever object he fancies that day. "That sure is a nice nerf gun. Isn't that a nice gun? Woo hoo! Sure would be nice to have a gun like that!" He wouldn't be so rude as to ask you directly to buy it for him. But with his incessant and adorable hinting, it's hard to resist. After all, can a guy ever have too many nerf guns or Disney stuffed animals?

Timmy holding his niece and nephew (Kaley and Colby) on one of "Sirs" airplanes.

# Timmy's Take on Trust and Fear

# "I'm Sir's copilot, you know!"

While most of us would prefer to fly in a large commercial aircraft, rather than a small two-seater plane… not Timmy. Timmy doesn't like flying in big jets, but always loved flying with our Father in his small "experimental" aircrafts. Timmy was Sir's copilot in every plane he ever flew, even the tiniest ones that looked more like large toys than legitimate aircraft. It wasn't the planes he trusted, but rather the pilot. Timmy put absolute trust in our Father's abilities to protect him.

Dad hung up his wings a few years back, but even to this day if you ask anyone at the Decatur, Illinois airport about Norman and Tim, they are legendary! You never saw one without the other. And that is still true today.

# "Ouch ... what did you do that for, Sir?"

Sir and Timmy used to do maintenance on apartment buildings he owned. Once, Sir had to climb 20 feet up on an old rickety ladder to work on the roof. Timmy, his ever-willing coworker, stood at the base of the ladder to hold it steady. But, as Sir began his descent, he missed a rung and plummeted down, landing right on top of Timmy! Timmy was none too happy about it either. "Ouch! What did you do that for, SIR?!!!" he complained. But despite the pain, when he realized that he had probably saved Sir's life, he was very happy to have broken his fall!

# "You are such a nice policeman. I like your badge!"

For many years, it was a common sight to see Sir (5 foot 8 inches - 150 pounds) driving the motorcycle, with Timmy (6 foot - 200 pounds) riding on the back. Sir has a "need for speed!" and, as a result, he encountered the police a few times, much to Timmy's dismay. Timmy is not scared of much, but he has a healthy respect for policemen. He doesn't know what lands you in jail, but he's not about to find out! He also has a tendency to compliment people when he is in an uncomfortable situation.

So, when Sir was pulled over by the police, Timmy would immediately jump off the bike, nervously shaking his hands, and proceed to give the police officer a big hug, saying "You are a nice policeman. I like your badge. That sure is a nice car. See Sir, he is a nice guy!" The police are usually so taken aback by this exchange that, to our knowledge, Sir has never gotten a speeding ticket. (I imagine this little scene has given local policemen a few laughs over the years as well!)

# "Roarrrrrrrrrrr!"

One time, Timmy and a dozen or so of our family went for a hike in the higher elevations of the Rocky Mountains. Suddenly, about 40 feet ahead, a very sizable black bear crossed the trail. Everybody turned tail and ran like crazy. All except Timmy. Timmy walked forward confidently, making a loud bear sound,

"Roarrrrrrrrrrrr!"

We all reacted with unbridled fear! But, Timmy wasn't scared. He didn't appear nervous in the least. For Timmy, encountering a bear seemed as natural as seeing a bird, and it turns out Timmy did the right thing. When you see a bear, act BIG and make loud noises! And it worked…as the bear turned and slowly sauntered back into the woods.

# "I don't want to go to Chicago"

One year Timmy participated in the Special Olympics, throwing the shot put. Because of his strength, he could throw it further than anyone else in the games. But when it came time to compete in the regional contest, whose winners would travel to national competition in Chicago, Timmy stepped up to the line and intentionally "dropped" the shot, lobbing it only a few feet. Baffled, Sir asked, "Timmy, what happened? You can throw it a lot further than that!!" To which Timmy replied, "I don't want to go to Chicago!"

Timmy was confident enough. He didn't need a gold metal to boost his ego, and he didn't want to fly. And, that was that. "NO THANKS!" he said, as he often does when he decides he absolutely does NOT want to do something!

# "I'm not scared of monsters."

Timmy's Uncle Billy, who also has Fragile X, had a vivid fear of monsters.

Once, Sir overheard Uncle Billy and Timmy talking about it. Uncle Billy said, "Tim, are you scared of monsters?" Timmy replied, "Don't know as I ever saw one!" For Timmy, it was all so simple. Why would you be afraid of something you've never seen? That's just silly.

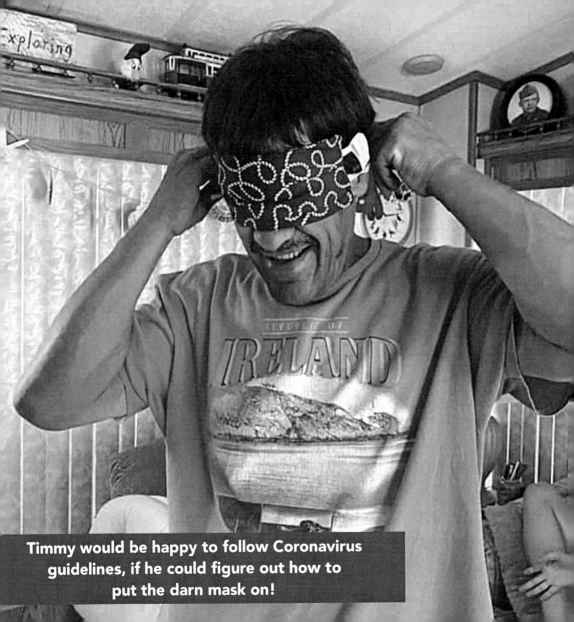

Timmy would be happy to follow Coronavirus guidelines, if he could figure out how to put the darn mask on!

# Timmy's Take on What Is Frustrating

# "I think we should impeach the Coronavirus!"

That was Timmy's solution to handle this pandemic we are facing during the writing of this book. Timmy is frustrated that he can't go with Mommy to stores and the beach. He can't even get into the pool. He doesn't exactly know what impeaching is, but, he does know that if a politician is causing trouble, "impeaching" is the word they use to get him out of office. So, if the Coronavirus is causing us trouble, we should just impeach it!

# "You Baboon!"

That's your name when you have pushed Timmy beyond what he can bear! Timmy will loudly declare, "YOU BABOON!" Immediately, he feels badly and apologizes. But if you don't quickly correct the attitude or actions that earned you the Baboon label, you'll most likely be called it again (especally if you forget to put your seatbelt on). Of course he'll apologize again. But the cycle of insult and apology won't stop until you rightly change your behavior.

# "They cheat!"

Timmy announces this almost every time he sees someone flying a private airplane or sailing a boat. It's his conclusion when anyone is having more fun than he is at that moment. They must be cheating! If he drives by a beautiful mansion, "They cheat." Or, maybe he spots someone lounging on a hammock with a Coke in hand, "they cheat." Of course, he's not angry. He's just certain that no matter who this person is or how hard they worked for this experience, they must have cheated, because he is not having as much fun in that moment as they are! Curiously, he never says that he cheats when he is the one having fun!

# "He talks too much.
# He's retarded you know!"

Our cousin, Craig Dean, is also affected by Fragile X. Craig and Timmy are similar in abilities, yet quite different in personality. While Timmy likes a good conversation, Craig LOVES to talk … a lot! When they visit with each other, they often sit and converse for hours, each one speaking about different subjects the entire time.

One time, Timmy was informed Craig was coming for a visit. But, when Craig arrived, we couldn't find Timmy. Maybe he just wasn't in the mood to talk that day. But when we found him and asked why he wasn't visiting, he replied matter-of-factly, "Craig talks too much." Then, as if letting us in on a little secret, Timmy said, "He's retarded you know!"

# "I gave that up!
# That's embarrassing!"

When Timmy was young, he would often bite his hand when frustrated, or in large crowds. Despite our efforts, we couldn't get him to stop. He would also chew his shirt if he was really nervous, and, in big crowds, he would "fly" by waving his hands high in the air. As he grew older, all these behaviors stopped, except one. He still waves his hands when he is nervous or excited. But, now it is at the side of his legs. If you ask him about any of these actions, he'll just say, "I gave that up! It's too embarrassing."

# "If you are going to fight, then don't fight at all!"

Like most siblings, my children squabbled quite often when they were young. For Timmy, such conflict was, and is, a definite no-no. As conflict brews, he is quick to offer his council, "If you are going to fight, then don't fight at all." Timmy doesn't treat anyone badly and can't understand why anyone ever would. If Timmy's first advice isn't heeded, and tensions and voices escalate, he'll try a different approach, advising, "If you're gonna fight, take it outside." He might not be able to get the argument to end, but at least he can get it far away from him!

The Hawbaker 6 in the early 1970s.

# Timmy's Take on Telling the Truth
## (No Matter What)

# "Who'd want to see your naked body!"

After a shower one day, I wrapped a towel around my body, ready to run through the family room to my bedroom. I yelled out, "Timmy, don't look … I have a towel on … turn your head." Without looking up or missing a beat, he very incredulously stated, "who would want to see your naked body!" You can always count on Timmy to give you his honest perspective, whether it's something you want to hear or not!

# "It's good enough for who it's for!"

Before going into full-time ministry, our family friends, Bill and Luann, moved to Luann's parents' very cramped basement to save money. When we went for a visit, we noticed the apparent downgrade from the nice big home they moved from. But of course, nobody wanted to comment … except Timmy. He looked around, took it all in, and said, "Well…it's good enough for Bill!"

Timmy has his standards, and if he doesn't think something is up to par, he'll let you know with a "It's good enough for who it's for."

# "Sure beats starvin' to death!"

For Mommy and Sir's 50th wedding anniversary, our family embarked on a cruise to celebrate! It was quite the luxury for all of us, especially when it comes to the lavishly prepared and beautifully presented food on board.

One night, as we enjoyed our gourmet meal of lobster and steak, we asked Timmy what he thought of the dinner. "Sure beats starvin' to death!", he declared. And, boy…was he right!

Timmy and Sir, the pilot and co-pilot

# From Sir's Viewpoint

(Written by our Father, Norman Hawbaker)

When we were dating, I knew Joyce's family had disabilities, but my love for her overcame any reservations I might have had in passing on any inherited traits to our children. So, when I realized that our third child, Timmy, was mentally affected, I initially felt sadness.

I thought about the many things I would never be able to do with my son. However, over time, those feelings were offset by all the fun things we COULD and DID do together. For many years, I was a private pilot and Timmy was always my copilot. I seldom went to the airport without Tim. He knew the airplanes and runways by heart, and we worked together doing many home repairs. Timmy even saved my life once. As my wife Joyce and I age, Timmy provides so much companionship and help. Most of the time, it's us, "the Three Amigos," doing everything together, along with our little Pomeranian, Roxie. We laugh a lot. We enjoy our lives. I truly don't know what we would do without Timmy!"

Mommy with her "chubby, yummy" baby, Timmy Lynn.

# From Mommy's Viewpoint

(Written by our Mother, Joyce Hawbaker)

As I looked around my family, I realized that there was a great possibility I might have a mentally challenged child. So, when our third child was born a boy, I was prepared and watched for the signs. Timmy developed slowly. It took a long time for him to be able to hold his head up and to sit up all by himself. He was delayed in everything, except smiling. He was a beautiful baby, with a round face, big dimples, and chubby hands and feet. He was, and is, adorable! As he was growing up, "Special Education" school was really fun for Timmy, because everyone there was like him. He played basketball and even got a crush on a girl, he called his "woman". Ha

It seemed as if the more Timmy lagged behind academically, the more he excelled socially. Everybody has always loved Timmy, and I have always been proud to be his mother. When all three of our girls got married, we didn't have to face "empty nest" syndrome, as we still had, and will always have, our special little boy, Timmy.

with nieces and nephews

with sisters, Brenda, Pam, and Connie

With niece, Millie Tzen

dancing with Manisha

with Cris Valdez

with Nephew, Jacob

# his fan club

holding niece, Aurora

with Grandma Hawbaker

with Janet and Emmitt Neary

with Brenda

with his little sister, Connie Jo

with sister, Pam (Paddi)

with nephew, Colby

with Jim and Marianne See

pulling nephew, Amos

Timmy and Brenda "livin it up" in Mexico!

# Brenda's Conclusion

In the gospel of Matthew, Jesus says, "the first will be last and the last will be first." Being Timmy's sister has given me a strong visual for that verse. When I picture heaven, I envision all the "special" children, seated at a massive banquet table.

Most weren't viewed as intelligent or significant when they lived in this world, but here they are celebrities. Jesus is at the head of the table having lively and deep conversations with Timmy, Billy, Craig, Justin, and many others like them.

They are whole and perfect. Many of us are in line waiting to be seated, and the "special" ones invite us to join them. (It seems there is always room at the table when the "least" are invited first.)

If we are measured by our love, Timmy will surely be among the first to be "rewarded" in heaven. The Father delights over these children who the world considers disposable.

In many countries, they are often teased, mocked, ridiculed, and even thrown out or abandoned. In the United States, and Western society, they are often aborted.

The Bible says that the "pure in heart will see God." If so, then Timmy has a spectacular view. Often when Timmy is frustrated, Mother will say, "did you pray?" and he replies, "always do!" And, I believe he does.

On earth, his prayers would never be written down in a liturgical book or a daily devotional. But, I imagine when Timmy's stories are told in heaven, everyone stands and applauds!

I am very confident that when that final day comes, Timmy will hear Jesus say, "Well done good and faithful servant! You have been faithful over little. I will set you over much. Enter into the joy of your Master."

Or maybe Jesus will speak in words Timmy might better understand,

"Timmy, you have led a gorgeous, sexy life! Now it is your turn to cheat. Come be my copilot and enter into the Lord's house ... and tell your friends and family, 'Sure! I'll save you a place at the table!'"

**brenda hawbaker lewis** has been in full-time ministry since 1992: Last Days Ministries, Mercy Ships, and YWAM Axiom. She has been privileged to travel the world, speaking and teaching on "Living the Dream."

In 2005, Brenda founded Child Restoration, International to help rescue children at risk of sexual exploitation

and trafficking in Asia. It continues to be one of the greatest privileges of her life.

When not on the road, Brenda is in Lafayette, Colorado, to be near her children, eight grandchildren (and counting), and her favorite hiking destination, the Rocky Mountains!